# North Africa

# NORTH AFRICA

By Mario Rossi

WITH PHOTOGRAPHS BY THE AUTHOR

Doubleday & Company, Inc./Garden City, New York

ISBN: 0-385-07706-8 TRADE
    0-385-02198-4 PREBOUND
LIBRARY OF CONGRESS CATALOG CARD NUMBER 73–18778
COPYRIGHT © 1974 BY MARIO ROSSI
ALL RIGHTS RESERVED
PRINTED IN THE UNITED STATES OF AMERICA
FIRST EDITION

For my son Richard

# North Africa

ACCORDING TO THE LEGEND, what is today North Africa was in prehistoric times, long long ago, part of Europe. This legend finds corroboration in recent scientific views according to which some 200,000,000 million years ago, when man had not yet appeared on this earth, the continents were fitted together in a single huge land mass. Africa was apparently slanted in such a way that its north part touched at one extremity Europe and on the other the North American continent. When the continents drifted apart, the northeastern part of Africa became attached to the Middle East, thus locking in a sea that before then had been part of the Pacific Ocean. And this is how the Mediterranean was born.

No sea in the whole world has witnessed as much history as the Mediterranean. Just think of it: three great historical religions were born around its rim—Judaism, Christianity, Islam —the glory that was Greece, the power that was Rome. And along those fateful shores lies also the Maghreb, a land comprising three countries: Tunisia, Algeria, and Morocco. The eastern end of the Maghreb overlooks Sicily and southern Italy while the western end is separated from Europe by the narrow Strait of Gibraltar. Beyond the Strait, the Maghreb faces the Atlantic, and, across that ocean, the United States.

In this ancient land many civilizations have left an imprint. Strangely enough, the least significant was that of Black Africa. Between the Maghreb and the rest of the continent lies the immense expanse of the Sahara, meaning "desert" in Arabic. The desert is not like the sea that joins peoples from faraway places.

I

Bedouins, the original inhabitants of North Africa, still live under tents.
They are mostly shepherds and traders.

It represents a barrier difficult to cross. Today, of course, we have trucks and planes that leap over the highest mountains and the vastness of the oceans. They can easily conquer the desert too. But until a few decades ago, only caravans of Bedouins (wandering desert tribes) and camels could brave the sandy dunes that roll softly until they disappear beyond the horizon.

No barrier existed, though, between North Africa and Europe to the north or the Arab world to the east. On the contrary, East met West in the Maghreb—and the impact was considerable, and mutual.

At one time, North African peoples later joined by Arabs invaded southern Portugal and southern Spain and ruled over these lands for a long period. They left behind some extraordinary examples of Moorish art and architecture of which the Europeans are justly proud. Later in history, they were in turn invaded by the same peoples they had once conquered. The history of the Maghreb has thus been closely interwoven with that of Europe. With rather brutal methods, which we today judge severely but which caused little scandal at the time, Europe forced the twentieth century upon the region. That meant not only the benefits of what we consider progress; but also the principles of the American and French Revolutions which, once assimilated, were used by North Africans to justify their struggle against continued European presence. It was thus in the name of Western principles that the Maghreb fought the West.

Even stronger than the European influence was that from the area we today call the Middle East. The Arab conquest in the eighth century resulted in the adoption by the North Africans of Arabic as their language and Islam as their religion. These were powerful instruments the North Africans selected—when they were not forced upon them—to express more fully their personality.

The Arabs, coming from the East, called Djezyra el-Maghreb

4

(island of the West) the lands they found as they advanced beyond Egypt. Their name for present-day North Africa is more than symbolic. The region possesses that uncompromising attachment to traditions and suspicion of all that is foreign typical of insular countries. Incidentally, Africa was the name the Romans gave to a province in the northeastern part of Tunisia. It was only much later that the name applied to the continent as a whole.

Geography helps explain the insularity of the peoples of the Maghreb. The region is traversed by a formidable series of mountains, from the Atlas in southern Morocco to the Aures system in eastern Tunisia. These mountains are filled with valleys and gorges that contributed to division into compartments and isolation. They were never permanently occupied by foreign conquerors, who settled in the fertile plains between the mountains and the sea. The people living in the mountains, and the valleys below, had little contact with outsiders. The French made no effort to colonize them. There are no navigable rivers to create links between valley and valley. Before the age of the airplane, the only connection with the outer world was the Mediterranean. It nourished commerce, piracy, and conquests.

The population of· the Maghreb is estimated at 33,000,000— about 15,000,000 in Morocco, 13,000,000 in Algeria, and 5,000,000 in Tunisia. Before independence there also were nearly 2,000,000 Europeans, mostly French. Population increase is a major problem in the Maghreb as in most of the underdeveloped world. Algeria, for example, had approximately 2,000,000 inhabitants at the time of the French occupation in 1830. That figure could be ten times as great by 1980. A visitor to North Africa becomes quickly aware of the magnitude of the problem. The streets and the squares are teeming with children, especially very young ones. Unfortunately, there are not yet enough schools for all of them.

The same people have inhabited North Africa since the dawn

*A caravan. The Bedouins move from place to place on camels and donkeys carrying the tents and provisions with them.*

of history. The Romans called them "Barbarians," from which "Berber" was later derived by the Arabs themselves. All peoples who did not partake of Roman civilization were referred to as "Barbarians." Even though North Africa was invaded a number of times, and often subjected to long periods of foreign occupation, it always remained true to itself. As the French historian Ch.-André Julien said, "The successive civilizations coming from the outside have been for the Berbers like outer garments under which body and soul have remained unchanged." Basically the same traditions, customs, and institutions have persisted throughout history, independently of historical vicissitudes. They are being remembered in festivals of which there are many at every season throughout North Africa.

These festivals are especially colorful in Morocco. They often represent the homage of a town to its patron saint. The women exhibit splendid multicolored robes, dance slowly, breaking the silence by a piercing cry. The men play their drums and sing. This is the Awashe, danced in the valleys of the Great Atlas. Celebrated in illustrations and photographs are the charges by mounted tribesmen displaying their skill, their finely chiseled guns, and the rich harnesses of their mounts. They are fearless horsemen.

The Tunisians have a long tradition of folkloric dances, of various origins and reflecting regional or tribal mores. Recently they have developed a popular theater which reflects often dramatically the life of the people. The Algerians are now trying to revive the folklore of their past, but their task is more difficult because during the 130 years of French administration they were forced to pretend they never had a past!

Folklore often reflects the influence of foreign conquerors upon the life of a people. There have been many migrations into North Africa, but never on such a large scale as to change the ethnic structure of the region. The Arab invaders, for example,

*Poorly lit stores line this pebbled street in the capital city of Rabat.*

did not number more than a few hundred thousand. Until relatively recent times the Berbers joined in tribes which often federated under the leadership of a prestigious chief. The concept of nation was unknown to them.

The Berbers were farmers and shepherds; their religion, before their conversion to Islam, animistic. They stood in awe of the forces of nature, which they tried to appease through magic rites. They revered the animals, the trees, the waters, and the grottos. Some of the ancient animistic rites have been preserved.

The region was nominally Christian during the final period of Roman occupation and later under the Byzantines. It produced holy men and scholars such as Saint Cyprian and Tertullian. A giant among the Church fathers, Saint Augustine, was born there. But Romans and Byzantines lived primarily in towns on the coast. Most Berbers did not. They were nomadic or semi-nomadic, moving their tents from place to place. Thus only a minority of the population felt the impact of Roman civilization and the Christian religion that followed, growing upon the ruins of the empire. As the towns were few and far between, Christianity was dispersed. Internal quarrels hastened a process of desegregation. Some scattered communities survived until the middle of the twelfth century. Then Christians were given the choice of conversion or execution.

Islam succeeded where Christianity had failed. It proved far more accessible to the Berber tribes, still very primitive at the time. The Berbers could make neither head nor tail of the extremely involved quarrels about doctrine that upset eastern Christianity. By comparison Islam is the simplest religion possible. It stands on "five pillars": (1) Profession of faith summed up in the Koranic formula "No God, whatsoever but Allah; Mohammed is the messenger of Allah." Acceptance of this formula is all that is required for a person to be a Moslem. (2) Prayer, five times daily with the face turned toward the holy city of Mecca.

(3) Alms giving, mainly to aid the poor. (4) Fasting; during a month the believer will abstain from food and drink from dawn till sunset. (5) Pilgrimage to Mecca, once in a lifetime.

The reasons for the conversion of the Berbers to Islam are not exclusively, perhaps not even primarily, religious. One of the main factors is that while the Romans and the Byzantines were total strangers a certain ethnic affinity existed with the Arabs. In prehistoric times the Berbers probably were of the same stock as the Semites. The Phoenicians who colonized parts of present-day Tunisia long before the arrival of the Arabs are believed to have come from what is today Lebanon in the Middle East. The Semitic Arabs thus were closely related to the Phoenicians and distant cousins of the Berbers. Their mentality and way of life must have been very accessible to the people they were conquering. This affinity helps explain the speed with which the Arabs converted the Berbers to Islam and made them adopt their language. When, many centuries later, Christians appeared along the coasts of North Africa, Islam became also an instrument for the preservation of a way of life and an identity. It became more strict and orthodox as the pressure from Christian Europe increased.

An important aspect of Islam that played a large role in the life of North Africa is mysticism. Its adherents are called Sufis. Their name derives from the woolen robe they wear called "souf" in Arabic. The Sufis live in monasteries which also serve as schools and hostels. The head of the monastery is called "Sheik" and he is said to possess the "baraka"—that is, a God-given power to perform miracles. Mysticism developed in Islam the cult of the Saints and of other faithfuls who by their virtue deserve to become known as "Friends of Allah." The latter, called Marabouts, are like monks living in hermitages. The orthodox opposed the mystics, whom they considered perverters of the original faith of Islam. The struggle had also a political connotation. The orthodox felt the Marabouts, by keeping the people in ignorance and encouraging the survival of paganism and animalism, were impeding social progress and delaying North Africa's progress.

The main possession that the peoples of North Africa have in common is their language. A language is not only a form of communication but the mirror of a culture. A person speaking a given language absorbs much of the civilization from which it sprang. The Arab-speaking people all feel themselves to be part of the same family, irrespective of ethnic origin. Arab is not a "race" or a religion—many Arabs are Christian—it is rather a sentiment, a feeling, a belonging to a culture, a sharing of the ways of thought of other peoples expressing themselves in the same idiom. Even though the North Africans often go to great length in stressing their differences from, say, the Egyptians, they refer to themselves as Arabs. The three countries have joined the Arab League, but are not very active participants. They also follow closely the Palestine problem while showing less emotional involvement than the eastern Arabs. Algeria is the most concerned because, being the only Arab country with a large colony in Europe—more than 700,000 Algerians live in France—it was also the only one whose people were exposed to scorn by some Europeans after Israel defeated the Arab armies in 1967.

The North Africans are late arrivals to Arab nationalism. Their countries are far from the main centers of Arab life and culture. During the period of French occupation they had been subjected to efforts to abandon Arabic and adopt French. Furthermore, the Europeans made their presence felt much earlier in North Africa than in the Arab east, and the long history of emotional contacts with Europe influenced the cultural development of the region.

It is probably too early to assess fully the impact of Europe on North Africa. For this region, as for the other parts of the world that have been colonized, the balance sheet shows a mixture of good and bad. It is useless at this point to try to determine whether North Africa would have fared better had Europe kept away from its shores. Europe didn't, so we had better stick to historical realities rather than suppositions. It is also a fact, even though most people in Africa and Asia would deny it vigorously, that Europe, at the time it undertook its colonizing effort, was sincerely thinking it was performing a civilizing mission. The search for raw materials to serve the developing industry in Europe was of course a very important factor. But Europe could most probably have obtained these materials even without occupying the countries producing them and turning them into colonies. Furthermore, in North Africa, at least at the time of the conquest, there were no raw materials of much interest to France. The historical record at the time shows rather conclusively that France was more interested in the region for reasons of prestige and to increase its power. Many Frenchmen believed they were bringing the benefits of "civilization" to the occupied countries. The Europeans had inherited the Roman concept that those who did not partake of their civilization were outside the pale, more or less barbarians.

The religious element must also be considered. Since the time of the Crusades, the first of which began nearly a thousand years ago, Christianity had tried to expel the "infidels" from the cradle of Christianity, the Holy Land. And for many centuries Europe fought the expansion of Islam represented by the Moslem conquest in Spain, France, and Sicily in the west and by the Ottoman Empire in the east. But Christians had no more success in converting many Moslems than Moslems had in converting many Christians. There had been conversions on both sides, but their effect was not lasting. Christianity introduced the Holy Inquisition in Western Europe, Spain especially, to weed out all traces of Moslem influence. The Moslems proved equally intolerant toward Christians. Each side was actually trying to preserve an identity, a historical heritage, against the encroachments of the other. In North Africa, for example, some of the most beautiful and ancient mosques were transformed by the French into Roman Catholic cathedrals. In Algeria, where the French represented merely a tenth of the population, there were more churches than mosques. Immediately after independence and the departure of the European population the churches were transformed into Moslem places of worship.

The aspect of European civilization that proved successful was the one the colonizers had hoped would never reach the shores of North Africa. The young people who were encouraged to forget Arabic and to study French were thus able to read such "subversive" documents as the American Declaration of Independence and the French Declaration of the Rights of Man. Up to the time of the French conquest, the North Africans had lived a traditional and conventional life that had changed but little since the Middle Ages. Contact with the West kindled an intellectual spark that set the region and the rest of the Arab world on fire. Referring to Western influence upon the Arab world in the period between the two World Wars, a distinguished Arab scholar, Phillip K. Hitti, wrote: "The Arab peoples at this time presented a seeming paradox: resisting with one arm European advances while with the other receiving and adopting European ideals and techniques. The new acquisitions from Europe were utilized in the fight against Europeans. Of the numberless novel ideas imported from the West, nationalism and political democracy were undoubtedly the most powerful. The espousal of nationalism encouraged the principle of self-determination and both led to the struggle for independence from foreign rule."

The extent of material progress introduced by the West is another subject of debate. The French feel they left behind an imposing testimonial of their "civilizing mission." Material progress, however, was intended primarily for the French "colons" who settled in North Africa. They took the best lands and exploited them in order to profit themselves and not the North

*The Great Mosque in the old town of Algiers was built in the
fourteenth century.*

African economy. Industry was not introduced, because the French felt they could furnish the North Africans with all the goods they required. For that reason the standard of living of the Moslem population is still quite low. The French also neglected mass education and as a result illiteracy is almost as high as it had been before the French arrived. Another problem, which the North Africans have in common, is the very high proportion of young people in the total population. It is extremely difficult to get them some sort of training and to find jobs for them.

On the positive side it must be recognized that by disrupting many stagnating customs, Europe contributed decisively to North Africa's entering the twentieth century. Even some of the traditional Moslem concepts were revised or modernized under the impact of the West. The process brought problems in its wake, but they were inevitable. The mentality of the people was changed in many significant respects. The present leaders of North Africa are among those who felt most deeply the impact of the West. The influence is evident in the way they try to awaken a national consciousness in their peoples.

Unfortunately the West was less thorough in introducing a modern way of life than in destroying the structures of the past. The young and the intellectuals feel most keenly the drama of a life suspended halfway between the past and the present, especially when the former expresses a tradition to which he belongs but that the latter forces him either to reject or radically to transform. The young Algerian, for example, was not so completely changed by the French that he became a Frenchman, but he was changed enough so that he began to feel alien in the traditional society that had survived French colonization.

The countries of the Maghreb became independent within the borders drawn by the French. Frictions in contested areas were on the whole resolved peacefully. The only exception was a brief armed clash between Algerians and Moroccans in 1963.

But North Africans are increasingly looking to what unites them, rather than to what divides them. Many of them feel that the Maghreb should represent one single unit.

The advocates of a greater Maghreb believe that, by uniting, the region could become a powerful political entity in world affairs. They point out that Tunisia, Algeria, and Morocco are geographically contiguous, speak the same language, profess the same religion, have had a similar colonial experience, have reached comparable stages of development, were exposed to the impact of the West at about the same time, under the common denominator of France, its language and civilization, and have economies that could become complementary to and that are largely oriented toward Western Europe's.

The Union could be gradual and merely economic at first. A form of political integration could follow later. This is not a vague dream. People are talking about it in earnest. Some preliminary steps have been made by the countries concerned. Upon its success or failure will hang much of North Africa's future.

TUNISIA IS THE SMALLEST of the three Maghreb countries but also the one with the longest history. It has 750 miles of coast on the Mediterranean. Its past has felt deeply the impact of the sea. Other peoples and civilizations have left a deep mark. The sea is an important vehicle for commerce and as a consequence Tunisia has a rather important middle class. The number of people who attended school and know how to read and write, or who have gone to the university, is much higher than in the rest of North Africa.

One is made aware of this difference by a visit to the cities of Tunisia. Take the capital, Tunis, for example. It is really many cities in one. In the southeast are the remains of a Roman aqueduct. That is not strange, considering that Tunis was once rebuilt by the Romans. The Arab impact is quite evident in the Souk—the town's market. It is something you are not likely to see anywhere else in the world. It consists of an area surrounded by a wall and crisscrossed by small busy streets. On those streets there are stores, one after the other, hundreds of them. They sell Tunisian handicrafts: beautiful rugs, silver objects, some of them very old, women's jewelry, intricate bird cages, women's and men's clothes, typical of the region, arms such as guns and swords, lovely laces, mint tea services. Needless to say, the Souk is the favorite place of visitors and foreigners, not only because of the products but also of the folklore. Right in the heart of the Souk lies a very beautiful ancient mosque and farther beyond a huge palace where the President of the Republic and some of his ministers have their offices.

The Tunisian flag seen here in Tunis has a crescent and a star on a red background. The crescent is the symbol of Islam.

*Monastir, an ancient fortified city of the Mediterranean, is the birthplace of Tunisia's first President, Habib Bourguiba.*

For many years a man has worked—more than any other—to make Tunisia what it is today. His name is Habib Bourguiba, the first President of Tunisia after it gained independence from France. He was born of a modest family, studied in Tunisia and then in France, and very early in life became deeply involved in politics. He began working for Tunisian independence at a time when this was considered just a wild dream. Both determination and moderation have characterized Bourguiba throughout his political career. He was determined that Tunisia should become independent, and he was equally determined, once independence was achieved, that his country should become a modern, progressive one. But the means he chose to achieve

22

those ends were as moderate as circumstances allowed. Whenever he had a choice between compromise and violence he chose compromise. He did not hesitate to use French advisers so that his country could progress sufficiently to become independent from French control. During the period of the Cold War he consistently sided with the West. Even though some people, especially the young, have resented Bourguiba's personal rule, and his impatience with criticism, everybody agrees that Tunisia owes an enormous debt to its first President.

Leaving the Presidential palace, and going back into the city, we find the modern sector built at the time of the French administration and the even more modern sector dating from independence. What was once the Bey's (the ruler's) palace now houses the National Assembly (roughly the equivalent of Congress) and also a very important museum, the Pardo. The museum contains remnants of the Roman rule over the country, especially mosaics—beautiful art works made from thousands of pieces of colored stones. These mosaics were once the floors of Roman villas and were covered over and preserved by sand through the centuries in perfect condition.

But long before there was a Tunis or even a Tunisia, the center of power in the region was the city of Carthage. Founded in 814 B.C., it is not the oldest city. Bizerta, for example, was founded in the year 1110 B.C. by Sicilians and Phoenicians. This is significant because it shows how very ancient is the influence of Europe and the Middle East. Bizerta became a naval base under the French and played an important role during World War II.

The Carthaginians were interested more in commerce than in military conquests. For that reason they stayed in the coastal area, where they built ports for their ships. The interior of the country remained under the authority of the Berber princes.

Carthage had a powerful rival—Rome. The two empires were locked in deadly combat from 264 to 146 B.C. After nearly

*Carthage, the city which defied the might of ancient Rome, was destroyed in the second century* B.C.

a century of struggle, broken by periods of uneasy peace, Carthage was vanquished. The Roman Senate ordered its total destruction. The territories formerly under its control were annexed by the Romans. With Julius Caesar begins the era of colonization. The Emperor Augustus ordered Carthage rebuilt in A.D. 14 and made it the capital of Roman Africa. But colonization spelled trouble. The Berbers rebelled and during seven years, led by a Prince named Jugurtha, they fought some of the Empire's best military commanders. Finally the Berbers were beaten and Rome ruled for various centuries, bringing peace and prosperity to the area.

The Romans, however, were unable to protect the frontiers of the Empire from the pressure exerted by the barbarians. The Germanic Vandals invaded France and Spain, crossed the Strait into Morocco, proceeded along the coast as far as Tripolitania, then headed north across the Mediterranean into Italy and Rome. The Empire collapsed in the West, but it survived in the East, with Byzantium (now Istanbul) as its capital. The Byzantine Emperor sent an expedition against the Vandals, who were routed in a decisive encounter near Tunis. Less than a century later, the last Byzantine governor in Africa was in turn beaten by the invading Arabs. Before rushing westward to the conquest of the rest of North Africa, the Arabs founded the city of Kairouan. It was built on flat land so that possible attackers could be spotted from far away. Kairouan is one of the most charming cities in North Africa and it is difficult to imagine that over a thousand years ago it was an armed camp.

Tunisia (called Ifriqya by the Arabs) with Kairouan as its capital became the military base for the several expeditions the Arabs undertook against the rest of the Maghreb and Spain. In 800, Ibrahim Ibm El Aghlab was placed at the head of the Tunisian government, with the right to transmit his power to his descendants. Beautiful mosques were erected in the main cities, but by far the most beautiful was that of Kairouan.

Few monuments have stirred the imagination and the emotion as much as this monument to a new religion. The French novelist Guy de Maupassant said, after a visit: "I know of only three religious buildings in the world that have given me the unexpected and shattering emotion that was aroused in me by this barbaric and astonishing monument: Mont-St.-Michel, St. Mark's in Venice, and the Palatine Chapel in Palermo. These three are the reasoned, studied, and admirable work of great architects sure of their effects, pious of course, but artistic first, inspired as much or more by their love of line, of form, and of decoration, as by their love of God. But at Kairouan it is something else. A race of fanatics, nomads scarcely able to build walls, coming to a land covered with the ruins left by their predecessors, picked up here and there whatever seemed most beautiful to them, and, in their turn, with these debris all of one style and one order, raised, under the guidance of heaven, a dwelling for their God, made of pieces torn from crumbling towns, but as perfect as the purest conceptions of the greatest workers in stone." Since ancient times, Arab chronicles gave an account of the founding of Kairouan that is shrouded in the miraculous.

A new Arab dynasty ruled the country for some time, then moved to Cairo, leaving behind a vassal. One of the latter's descendants broke with Cairo and proclaimed his independence. Cairo took revenge by unleashing an Egyptian tribe which invaded Tunisia, bringing devastation everywhere. Taking advantage of the anarchy that followed this invasion, the Almohads, who had established a strong empire in Morocco, occupied the rest of North Africa. They installed a government with Tunis as its capital in 1159. In 1229 the Almohad governor of Tunis proclaimed his independence from Morocco and founded a dynasty that was to rule for three and a half centuries.

In the sixteenth century Tunisia was conquered by two pirates—we shall meet them again in Algeria—and placed under

*A typical Tunisian store in Kairouan, founded in 671 by the Arab conqueror Sidi Okba for whom its Great Mosque is named.*

the authority of the Ottoman Empire. But Turkish rule was challenged by Emperor Charles V, who sent an army of thirty thousand Spaniards to Carthage. Some years later the Turks sent an expeditionary corps of their own into the country and chased out the Spaniards, whose presence had caused revolts and disorders everywhere. Tunisia became a Turkish province under a Bey (ruler). Even though the Beys soon became and felt like Tunisians, the period of nominal Turkish rule from the sixteenth century to the French conquest was one of anarchy and finally of financial bankruptcy.

Tunisia became a French protectorate in 1881. The country had a more integrated structure than either Algeria or Morocco. The split between towns and countryside was less dramatic than in Algeria, nor did Tunisia shut itself off completely from the West as did Morocco. The middle-class leaders of the towns had become aware of the need for modernization even before the arrival of the French. A constitutional movement, the first in the Arab world, was formed in 1856. It eventually inspired a nationalist movement—organized in 1920 —to which it gave its name: Destour (constitution). In 1934 the younger members of the Destour revolted against the intransigence of the older generation and formed their own movement, called Neo-Destour. They included Habib Bourguiba, Mongi Slim, who was to become his country's representative to the United Nations and President of the U.N. General Assembly, and Salah ben Yussef, with whom Bourguiba later broke after a bitter fight.

The Tunisian nationalist movement is important for a variety of reasons. It was fully developed by the time Morocco became a protectorate in 1912 and long before the Algerians rose in rebellion. It also became identified with tactics known as "Bourguibism"—roughly, negotiating and bringing pressure at the same time. The movement could grow as it did not only because it became identified with an articulate and intelligent middle class, but also because the French helped the country in a remarkable way. While the French were trying to deprive Algeria of an identity, in the vain hope of turning it into a French province, and were dealing in Morocco with a country several centuries behind the times, in Tunisia they were introducing the kind of reforms that were desperately needed. The administration was modernized and elected councils formed, the economic basis was developed, and many young Tunisians were allowed to complete their education in France.

The relations between Bourguiba and France had many ups and downs. In 1936 Bourguiba was in Paris negotiating with the newly formed Popular Front. In 1938 he was in prison—where he had been before and was to return again. He was still behind bars when the Germans arrived. Bourguiba refused to go along with the new masters as so many Mideast Arabs had done. To his wife and son who visited him in prison in August 1942 he said: "Tunisia must work with the democracies to the fullest . . . We can discuss independence after the war has been won." The Germans handed him over to the Italians hoping he would make a pro-Axis statement, but he refused.

The French returned after the defeat of the Axis in North Africa in 1943 and tried to re-establish their prewar position. Bourguiba sought in vain to work out an arrangement that would have enabled the Tunisians and the French to administer the country together. In 1945 he went to Cairo, but was disillusioned with the kind of atmosphere he found among the Arabs of the Middle East. He returned home in 1949, and the next year the French offered internal autonomy, or limited self-rule, and eventual independence. After one more year they changed their minds and began again persecuting the nationalists. Once more Bourguiba went to jail. But in 1954, with the arrival in power of Premier Pierre Mendès-France, the situation changed

*Tunisian women carrying hay to market.*

dramatically. The Tunisians first gained autonomy; then, in 1956, independence. In 1957 the monarchy was abolished and a Republic proclaimed, with Bourguiba as its first President.

The French, as we said, modernized Tunisia considerably. They kept the Bey in power and allowed him to have a government. The authority of the Beys was insignificant because they had to take orders from the French, but they served to preserve a sense of national identity for Tunisians. Today the country is probably one of the few in the underdeveloped world which comes closest to European standards. And today it probably feels closer to Europe than to Africa or the Middle East. With independence, internal divisions showed up more sharply. They surely were not as bad as Bourguiba liked to paint them in order to justify his absolute rule. In any case, they were accountable more to geography than to history.

The country is divided into three regions: the Tell to the north, the plains in the center, and the Sahara to the south. The Tell is where most Tunisian history has been enacted. The oldest and largest towns are there, and also the most fertile soil. In antiquity the region was the "granary of Rome." Most French "colons" settled there.

The central region includes part of the eastern coast and the lands behind. It comprises two rather important ports, Sousse and Sfax, and some lovely towns: Kairouan, Monastir with an ancient fort overlooking the sea, El Dyem known especially for a Roman colosseum, Mahdia with old white houses—a fishing town of unusual charm.

But as we leave the coast and proceed toward the interior we discover the ugly face of poverty. The condition is one of desolation and neglect. The olive tree is practically all that grows there. The rain seldom comes, and the land is parched by the sun, but when it does, sometimes it turns dry beds into furious rivers that bring destruction and desolation. One such

34

*A hotel at Hammamet on the Mediterranean coast. Hammamet has become a highly popular tourist center with Europeans.*

flood took place in 1969 and it had a disastrous effect on the country.

The villages betray the poverty of the region. But no matter how poor, how desolate the village, it has a school. Children, often in school uniform, which abolishes the difference between rich and poor, receive a very basic form of instruction.

The people of the region complain that if dikes and canals were built the land could be irrigated and become productive. They say the people from the cities keep all the money to themselves and neglect the countryside. The counter argument is that dikes and canals are very expensive to build and that there is simply not enough money to go around.

In an effort to increase the country's revenue and make more funds available for reforms, the Tunisian government has paid a great deal of attention to tourism. In recent years beautiful resorts have been built all along the Mediterranean which compete with the finest in Europe. Many Europeans are now taking their vacations in Tunisia. Distances have of course been cut considerably by the jet age. The flight between Tunis and Rome, for example, with the new jets recently introduced takes approximately half an hour. Modern luxury hotels have also been built in the main cities.

North of Kairouan, the central region is mostly highlands that yield barely enough grass for goats and camels to feed on. To the south of the ancient city, the lowlands extend all the way to the desert. The Sahara represents the southernmost part of the country. Only those who have wandered there in the vastness of the night, and have seen the moon among billions of stars, and its rays playing with the dunes, can understand its gripping beauty.

If I were asked which in my opinion is the loveliest spot in Tunisia I would unhesitatingly name Sidi Bou-Said. This little town perched on top of a hill overlooking the sea is close to Carthage and was obviously inhabited by wealthy people, because the houses and villas are truly magnificent. Sidi Bou-Said has become not only a tourist attraction but also an intellectual center. Many painters and writers—some from Europe and the United States—have made their home there.

*The Hotel Fourati at Hammamet, one of the most modern and best equipped in Tunisia.*

Another locality of rare charm, and with an aura of mystery, is the island of Jerba. According to an account by the greatest of Greek poets, Homer, dating back some three thousand years, Jerba was the island of the lotus-eaters where Ulysses landed with his men. In Greek legend the lotus was a plant whose fruit had the power to make men forget the reality of life. The present inhabitants of the island live a life not much different from that of their ancestors centuries and even millennia ago. Some of them belong to a Jewish community that is one of the oldest in the world. According to tradition, the first Jews of Jerba found asylum there after the destruction of Jerusalem by Nebuchadnezzar twenty-six centuries ago.

*Sidi Bou-Said, one of the loveliest spots on the Mediterranean looking down over the sea and the Gulf of Tunis, has become an artistic and cultural center.*

TO REALIZE HOW SHARP the differences can be among the three Maghreb countries, despite so many affinities, it is enough to step from Tunisia into Algeria.

Tunisia is about the size of the State of Washington; Algeria is nearly four times the size of Texas. Algeria was not so thoroughly colonized by Rome as Tunisia. The sea dominated the history of Tunisia; the mountains, the hills, and the valleys that of Algeria. French rule over Algeria lasted much longer: 132 years, compared to 75 years in Tunisia. Under the French, Tunisia enjoyed a certain degree of internal autonomy while Algeria was administered as a province of France. While Tunisia and Morocco were allowed to preserve an identity, the French spent well over a century trying to convince Algerians that they had no history. Every country or region has a past, but the Algerians were in fact told they had none and that their country had been no more than a geographical expression. Moslem children studied history from textbooks prepared for French children. According to those books Algerian history began with the French conquest.

When independence came in 1962, there was not a single history text that could be used in the schools. A commission had to be appointed to uncover the country's past. Algerians were also discouraged by the French from celebrating festivals or reviving in any manner their traditions and customs. It is indeed quite extraordinary that despite the most concentrated effort to deprive Algerians of their way of life, the country should have been ready to make immense sacrifices to reacquire a personality of its own.

How did it happen? The main reason probably stems from the impact of geography on Algerian history. Villages high up in the mountains or sheltered within steep ravines defied the sustained efforts of colonizers through the ages. No French "colon" went to live there. The inhabitants of those inhospitable regions were more or less left to themselves. They were to provide later the men and the terrain for a bitter and prolonged struggle. The Algerians have always been predominantly a people of farmers and shepherds—a people, that is, very close to the earth, very attached to traditions and to their religion. The inhabitants of the mountains and the valleys were, of course, also shielded from the influence of foreign civilizations. This is the reverse side of the coin. While they remained largely withdrawn within themselves, other countries, under the impact of commerce and the exchange of ideas, were achieving great progress. But Algerians were lagging behind.

This circumstance, plus the existence of physical obstacles to mutual contacts from which a national consciousness could emerge, meant that Algerians were not, at the time of the French conquest, a nation in the modern sense of the word. They developed a national consciousness as a reaction to French efforts to deprive them of a personality and during the long years of armed struggle for independence. Let us also remember that not too many peoples had a sense of national identity in 1830, especially in Africa and Asia.

The important factor in the Algerian background is a common land. Algeria has existed as a geographical entity since ancient times. It roughly corresponds to the Roman province of Numidia. With the rest of North Africa it was invaded by the Vandals and later ruled by the Byzantines. Its modern history begins when it became a part of the Ottoman Empire.

In the year 1518, two Ottoman corsairs of Greek origin, Khayr-al-Din Barbarossa and his brother, occupied Algeria after defeating the Spaniards, who had built isolated forts along

*In the Algerian countryside water is scarce and often must be carried for long distances.*

*Entrance to the mosque of El-Hamel in southern Algeria, where a distinguished Koranic school is held.*

the coast. Barbarossa gave Algeria to the Ottoman Emperor and was in exchange made Bey of Beys. He set up a military aristocracy backed by an Ottoman army of professional soldiers called Janissaries. He also organized a strong and well-equipped fleet which he placed at the orders of the Emperor in the pursuit of his imperial policy in the Mediterranean. In 1534 Barbarossa temporarily occupied Tunisia. That country became a Turkish province forty years later.

At that time Algeria was independent in all but name. The only form of dependence upon the Emperor was payment of an annual tribute. Its main activity then and during the three centuries that followed was piracy, primarily against the ships of Christian nations. Piracy was somehow justified as a holy war—Moslems against Christians—but it was in fact highly profitable, since it represented the main source of revenue to the State treasury. Algeria had indeed become the headquarters of sea robbers. The strongest powers, such as France and England, managed to impose respect for their flags. The smaller countries were compelled to seek safety in tribute. Among the smaller countries of the time which paid tribute regularly was the United States. In 1783, however, the United States decided that its flag, too, should be respected and waged war against Algeria. A few years later, in 1795, the two countries signed a treaty of peace and friendship.

The Ottoman Empire was organized for the primary purpose of carrying out warfare. It was thus not much interested in the welfare of the people over whom it ruled. Algeria had been divided into four provinces which enjoyed a large degree of autonomy. The Janissaries were taxing them heavily, however, and this led to repeated revolts. During the time it belonged to the Ottoman Empire the country had native or thoroughly assimilated rulers.

The French began occupying Algeria in 1830. The official reason was flimsy, as is usually the case in such circumstances.

*The Tombeau de la Chrétienne is an ancient monument near the Algerian coast showing likeness with Egyptian art. It has been considered since time immemorial as the mausoleum of a famous person, probably a woman, who lived in the pre-Islam era.*

*Skikda, formerly Philippeville, was built by the French upon the ruins of a Roman city destroyed by the Vandals in 533.*

The real reason was that the French government of the time was anxious to divert public opinion from the situation at home. Even though they were vastly underarmed, the Algerians rose to combat. Leader of the resistance was a young man of twenty-four called Abd-el-Kader. He led his men in a relentless war against the French until 1847, when he was compelled to surrender. In the process of conquering the country the French committed, alas, many atrocities. I will spare you the details,

*A little girl in the Casbah of Algiers smiles when photographed.*

which make pretty awful reading. The facts were recorded by the French themselves. With Abd-el-Kader out of the way the French were masters of most of Algeria. The resistance made its last stand in the mountains of Kabilya, an important chain to the southeast of Algiers. It was only in 1871 that an army of eighty-six thousand Frenchmen crushed that last bastion of independence. Algeria had become, as the French put it, "pacified." Resistance had lasted exactly forty years.

Gradually, more than a million Frenchmen settled in Algeria. The disparity between the French and the Moslem population was enormous. Half a million Algerians owned an average of 35 acres each, of which only 12.5 were productive, while twenty-five thousand Europeans owned an average of 270 acres each, of which 155 were productive. The proportion 155 to 12.5 is quite impressive! Furthermore, the French had the best lands, those nearest the coast, while seventy-five per cent of the land owned by the Moslems was inadequate for development. According to United Nations statistics, the average income among Algerians was slightly superior to that of India, which has one of the world's lowest. Industry was not developed because Algeria was meant to furnish France with raw materials and to become a market for French products. Unemployment was widespread. Hundreds of thousands of Algerians had to migrate to France, where they performed the most menial tasks. In 1954, out of two thousand civil servants in the central government only eight were Moslem. Even though the French had marvelous farms, built splendid roads, brought electricity throughout the country and the comforts of modern life to the cities, the overwhelming majority of the Algerian population led a life of poverty. It must be recognized, of course, that the improvements the French introduced for their own use now serve the Algerians.

Those Algerians who had come in closer contact with the French presence could not fail to be affected. After all, one Frenchman to every ten Algerians is a high proportion; it becomes even higher if one excludes the inhabitants of the mountain regions. The large cities gradually became more French

*Ancient Tepaza on the Algerian coast is one of several spots where the Romans settled at the time they ruled North Africa.*

*Constantine, originally called Cirta, was rebuilt in the fourth century by the Roman Emperor Constantine and named for him.*

*A building in the old city of Constantine.*

than Algerian. The universities were entirely French. The more educated Algerians could only express themselves in French; there is a distinguished literature of French-writing Algerian novelists and essayists. Even when they aimed to express the deepest emotions of their people, they had to do so in a "foreign" language.

Quite a few educated Algerians tried, in the period between the two World Wars, to reconcile their country and France, to rationalize the anomalous situation in which they found themselves. Because of the transforming contact with the West they had found the old traditions quite unfulfilling and inadequate. At the same time, try hard as they might, they could not be fully French. Here is but one dramatic example. In 1936 a distinguished Algerian wrote: "If I had discovered an Algerian nation, I would have become a nationalist and would not have been ashamed of it. Six million Muslims live on this soil which has been French for a hundred years. Out of this hungry mass, we shall make a modern society, elevate them to human dignity, so that they may be worthy of the name of Frenchmen." Twenty-two years later, the author of these lines, Ferhat Abbas, was to become Premier in the Provisional Government of the Algerian Republic.

World War II represented a decisive turning point in the history of Algeria. The wind of freedom that blew over Asia and Africa hit Algeria with full force. The moderates who had believed in integration with France now recognized it could never be achieved. They sought federal autonomy within the French system. In 1943 General Charles de Gaulle in a speech at Constantine promised the Muslims certain reforms. It was too late. The Algerians now wanted recognition as a nation. The "colons" urged the government to get tough. The country was heading for a crisis. On May 8, 1945, an event took place that was to represent "a point of no return." It was one of those dates that mark the lives of a people and put an end to an era. On that day Algerian nationalists, even the most moderate among them, lost confidence in France.

This is what had happened. At Sétif, during and shortly after a parade to celebrate the victory of the Allies, about a hundred Frenchmen were killed by Moslem extremists who vented their hatred for their foreign rulers by knifing and clubbing such settlers as they could find and raping European women. The reprisal was pitiless. The French cruiser *Duguay-Trouin* shelled the outskirts of Kerrata while American-built bombers flying hundreds of sorties blasted crowded Muslim housing areas off the map. This "punishment" cost forty thousand lives.

In the years that followed, Algerians were divided between those who, like Ferhat Abbas, advocated an Algerian state freely associated with France, and the followers of Messali Hadj who were for total independence. Paris often realized the danger of the situation, but at every turn constructive efforts were stymied by the "colons," the local administration, and the military. On the Algerian side the traditional leaders, including the fiery Messali Hadj who had done a great deal in awakening a nationalist consciousness among the people, were left behind by a younger generation of rebels who advocated a recourse to arms.

They began organizing in 1947 and by 1954 were ready for rebellion on a large scale. The Front of National Liberation (FLN) was born. Soon the rebellion assumed such proportions that France had to commit half a million soldiers in an effort to crush it. The war cost the French treasury one billion dollars a year. The struggle was brought to the attention of the United Nations, thus becoming an international issue. Evidence that torture was being used against the nationalists troubled the conscience of many Frenchmen. Soon France itself was on the verge of civil war. In 1958 the Fourth Republic was overthrown and General de Gaulle brought to power. The FLN tried to strengthen its position by forming a Provisional Govern-

Constantine. The movie poster underscores the contrast between the old and the new in this busy city built by the Romans.

ment of the Algerian Republic. As the situation became increasingly grave in both Algeria and France, de Gaulle and the FLN sought a way to get together and talk. A ceasefire was finally called in March 1962.

Algeria had become a free nation, but at a terrible price. One million Algerians had been killed, one person in ten; 300,000 refugees were in Morocco, Tunisia, and Libya; 150,000 persons had been in concentration camps.

President de Gaulle had committed his prestige in practically forcing his countrymen to accept Algerian independence. Despite all the bitterness and the suffering, the two countries soon agreed it was to their mutual advantage to forget the past and become friends. The French offered the new Algerian state massive financial and technical assistance. The Algerians, for their part, have warmer feelings toward the French today than ever before in their long history.

Unfortunately, no sooner had the country achieved independence than the FLN's leaders began fighting among themselves. The first President, Ahmed Ben Bella, was overthrown in a military coup that brought Colonel Houari Boumedienne to power.

Independence confronted Algeria with many assets and many liabilities. The main asset is its people—hardworking, industrious, determined to move out of their backwardness and into the modern world. Having been the only people in Africa who had to wage a long, bloody, and bitter struggle for their independence, they are determined not to waste what they have paid for so dearly. Another important asset is the country's wealth. Oil and natural gas found in large quantities in the desert and exported to various markets, including the United States, furnish the revenue with which to pay for the modernization of the country. Industry is developing rapidly. An agrarian reform has been introduced.

These are important assets, but the liabilities are also serious.

*Constantine. The ancient city built on a precipice defended itself fiercely against the French invaders in the nineteenth century.*

Under the French the education of the Algerians was badly neglected. The government tries hard to remedy the situation, but for the time being there simply are not enough men with the training required to fill the many new managerial posts in industry and government. Another important problem was the need to create new state structures from scratch. Having been treated as a province of France, Algeria lacked centralized structures such as survived in Tunisia and Morocco. The task, therefore, was not to transform an outdated government, but to create one out of nothing. The same applied to all other organs of government, such as the provincial and municipal administrations. The new Algeria also inherited enormous differences in development among regions.

Were it not for the vigor and dynamism that were unleashed by the struggle for national liberation, Algeria would be in a very tragic situation indeed. Everything indicates, instead, that if the present trends continue, it will modernize much faster than most other countries in Africa and Asia.

Algeria could make much more progress in developing tourism, which would be an important source of foreign exchange. Algeria is one of the most beautiful spots in the world. In my many travels I have rarely seen a coast of such indescribable grandeur as the "corniche" halfway between Algiers and the Tunisian border. Equally attractive, in an entirely different way, is the desert in the southernmost regions. There are the caravans, the same as have crossed its endless expanses for centuries, perhaps millennia, with Bedouins wearing the same style of dress, carrying the same goods, on the same kind of animals. But there are also the oil fields, the pipelines, the natural gas, the airfields, the modern hotels with air conditioning. And in this infinity of sand there are also islands of life, some of which are probably as old as life itself—the oases. Each is like a very small town, often fortified, with its market, flat-top houses, and a mosque.

*Veiled women. The veil is gradually being abandoned in the more modernized countries. It is still quite common in Morocco and Algeria.*

*Annabas (formerly Bone) is a busy port in eastern Algeria, the last important city on the Mediterranean before reaching Tunisia.*

*The new village of Tepaza on the Mediterranean was built to promote tourism, mostly European.*

North of the desert extend the vast regions that look like the American West; so much so that cowboy pictures have been filmed there. And then gradually one reaches the mountains and the valleys; the very regions, that is, where the traditions and the ancient ways of life were preserved intact.

Finally, close to the coast are the many cities, some quite old, like Constantine, so named after the Roman Emperor who conquered it, and Algiers, the capital, with its Casbah, a walled citadel on a hill. Around these ancient centers, the French built the cities of today. In the plains between the main cities the French also built a number of villages that look very much like those in Europe, with the main square, the monument to the war dead, the church—now transformed into a mosque—and the outdoor cafes.

IN MOROCCO differences from the rest of the Maghreb are far greater than those we recalled earlier between Algeria and Tunisia. Roman penetration was more superficial—witness the absence of notable monuments. The country never became part of the Ottoman Empire. It actually remained independent, despite Western encroachments along the coast, until the French occupation just prior to World War I. The impact of the Arab conquest was more far-reaching because it was through Morocco that Spain was conquered. As a result, Moroccan history is more complex, and we have already seen that at times it encompassed Tunisia and Algeria.

While closest to Europe, Morocco is also the Maghreb country that felt most strongly the impact of Black Africa. Its history reflects the conflicting claims of the Mediterranean north and the African south, as well as the contrast between the mountains and the plains.

The Far West (Maghrib al Aqsa) of the Arab world, Morocco was the Garden of the Hesperides to the ancient Greeks, who marveled at the sight of the "golden apples," their name for the oranges growing in the country's many groves. The area facing the Atlantic Ocean is flat land often breaking into low hills. This is where most of Morocco's history has been enacted. Beyond, crossing the country like a backbone, extend the mighty chains of the Atlas Mountains—the Middle, the High, and the Anti-Atlas. The Atlas represents a natural barrier that further divides Morocco from the rest of the Maghreb. Beyond the chain, "Outer Morocco" is an immense ex-

*View from Hassan Tower in Rabat. This tower is a twelfth-century minaret of the Almohad period, at the foot of which are visible a few columns of the ruins of the mosque Al-Mansur, planned to be the world's biggest but never completed.*

panse of sand and rocky plateaus of savage beauty. To the north of the country the Rif foothills guard the Mediterranean shore.

Between the Rif and the Middle Atlas, a corridor connects the shielded plains along the Atlantic with the rest of the Maghreb. And through that corridor came the Arab invasion at the end of the seventh century, with an irresistible force that only the barrier of the ocean could break. Soon it was diverted toward the north. In 711 a Berber freedman at the head of seven thousand troops, also Berber, erupted into Spain. He was Tariq ibn Ziyad, after whom Gibraltar (from Jabal Tariq, "Mount of Tariq") was named. Thus began a conquest that brought the Moslems all the way to France, where they were checked between Tours and Poitiers by Charles Martel. The battle, decisive for the history of Europe, was fought in 732, the year that marked the first centennial of Mohammed's death.

By that time Islam had reached the farthest corners of the known world. "One hundred years after the death of the founder of Islam," Professor Hitti wrote, "his followers were the masters of an empire greater than that of Rome at its zenith, an empire extending from the Bay of Biscay to the Indus and the confines of China and from the Aral Sea to the lower cataracts of the Nile, and the name of the prophet—son of Arabia joined with the name of almighty Allah—was being called five times a day from thousands of minarets scattered over southwestern Europe, northern Africa and western and central Asia."

Internal struggles among Arabs, competition between Arabs and Berbers, and wars against the Christians marked Moslem rule over Spain. It also brought a splendid civilization to a part of the world that was at the time underdeveloped and backward. Greatest progress was reached under the dynasty established by Abd-al-Rahman, an escapee from civil war in Spain. This dynasty with its capital in Córdoba lasted three centuries (736–1031). There followed a period of great political confusion,

*Tannery at Fez. Here leather is dyed and made ready for the artisans
to produce the fine leather objects for which Morocco is famous.*

*Fez. Most Moroccan families still get their water from public fountains. Note the delicate tile work characteristic of public fountains throughout North Africa.*

which resulted in the increase of Christian power in the north of Spain.

In 788 an Arab called Idriss ibn-Abdullah, another rebel against the caliphate (empire), arrived in Morocco and founded a dynasty. He took the title of Imam (religious leader) and rallied numerous tribes around him. He died of poison and became the Saint of Morocco. His son Idriss II gave Morocco its first capital, Fez. This oldest among imperial cities is to this day one of the loveliest in North Africa. Set among hills, Fez was to become the country's religious, political, and cultural center. It had a famed University and mosques built more than a thousand years ago. Fez is still largely like it must have been in medieval times. The narrow, muddy streets are lined with dark shops where artisans produce the handicrafts for which Morocco is famous. The city represented the Mediterranean north in the contest with the African south, the plains always threatened by the peoples of the mountains. It controlled the main arteries to the interior.

Fez's role was challenged when in the eleventh century warrior tribes from the south, the Almoravids, took power and founded another imperial city, Marrakesh. Called "the Pearl of the South," this legendary city is to this day a major center of attraction. The monuments that still exist are the work of succeeding dynasties. The Koutoubria mosque is famous for its minaret and the Ben Youssef medersa (school) for its mosaics, marbles, and carved woodwork. The melancholy Suadian Tombs are extraordinarily beautiful. Behind the city, the Ourika Valley offers a serene escape to green fields, and clear streams lined with fruit orchards where mimosa, lily of the valley, and carnations grow.

The Almoravid kings soon conquered the whole of Morocco, moved eastward as far as Algiers, then crossed the Strait into Spain to defeat the Christian kings. Morocco and Moslem Spain were united under a single rule. The empire extended from the

Ebro to the Niger, from the Atlantic to Algiers, and was never again to reach such proportions.

In the twelfth century, the Almoravids were followed by the Almohads. As was the case with the preceding dynasties, the new rulers fought their wars on religious as well as political grounds. The Almohads abandoned the Sudan to the south but extended their rule eastward to the Tunisian coast and to Libya as far as Tripoli. It was under this dynasty that diplomatic relations were established—apparently for the first time—with European countries. With the Almohads another famed city, Rabat, became a center of empire. Capital of modern Morocco, the city was then a military base—Ribat el Fath, the Camp of Victory. Its monumental gateways, intended to give a show of power, contrast with the many trees and gardens, gay and inviting.

After a period of anarchy the Merinids took power and held it for two centuries, during which they distinguished themselves more as patrons of the arts than as conquerors. They are remembered especially for the necropolis (ancient cemetery) of Chellah, with its ramparts within which a delicately etched minaret still stands. The Merinids founded yet another imperial city, Meknès. Enclosed by twenty-five miles of triple walls with bastions, with its gigantic Bat el Maussour gateway, it was designed primarily to station troops and store supplies. The Merinids were not as strong as their city looked. Far from it. And as a result of that weakness a series of events took place that were to mark the history of Morocco for centuries. Taking advantage of the situation, the Portuguese established several bases along the coast. From then on the history of Morocco consists mainly in the country's religious and national responses to the European presence.

It was now the turn of Europe gradually to dominate the areas from which it had been dominated. The Christian kings from their retreats in northern Spain had launched a "recon-

*Casbah des Oudaya, an ancient fortress named after the descendants of an Arab tribe which arrived in North Africa early in the thirteenth century. Part of the tribe was placed with its own caid in the casbah toward the end of the seventeenth century.*

*Meknès. Water vendors still do a brisk business in busy streets and markets to quench the thirst produced by the intense heat.*

quista" (reconquest) which by the middle of the thirteenth century left only Granada in Moslem hands. This last bastion was conquered in 1492, the year America was discovered. Gradually, all Moslems who had remained in Spain were expelled. Some three million people, including Spaniards who had converted to Islam, were banished or executed. Western encroachment in Morocco coincided with the establishment of Turkish power in Algeria and later Tunisia. It produced a deep suspicion of everything Western among the native population. This attitude eventually developed into a national psychosis that was to prove tragic, because it cut Morocco off from European learning and progress.

Self-defeating isolation was to characterize the history of Morocco during the centuries that followed. True, Morocco signed trade agreements with European powers and was among the first to recognize the independence of the United States of America. But these were superficial, formal contacts. The country shied away from the enormous changes the new era of colonial conquests brought to Europe. After developing a great civilization when Europe was enveloped in the obscurity of the Middle Ages, Morocco was to suffer the fate of countries that refuse to move with the times. When the French began its occupation in 1907, Morocco, ruled by an autocratic Sultan (king) and suffering from administrative incompetence, was unable to offer effective resistance.

The French put on the throne an obedient ruler of their choice and in 1912 established a protectorate over the country. It was to last forty-four years. Morocco was divided into three zones: French, Spanish, and International (Tangiers). The Moroccan Sahara had previously been divided between France and Spain.

The French and Spaniards were very soon to discover that to place a puppet at the head of a country does not mean to ensure its submission. Badly as their country was run, most Mo-

*Meknès, one of Morocco's imperial cities founded in the tenth century, was protected against invaders by huge stone walls.*

roccans saw no need for foreign "protection." The mountain tribes of the Middle Atlas were the first to rise up in arms. Soon they were joined by the Rif tribes under a legendary leader, Abdel Krim. Krim took on the Spaniards first and defeated them in a series of bloody encounters in 1921. Three years later the Spaniards, pressed by Krim toward the sea, were left with a few strong points along the Mediterranean coast. In 1925 Abdel Krim attacked the French in the direction of Fez. French and Spaniards joined forces for the occasion and some of the most brilliant generals of World War I were ordered to the scene to check the onrush of the fierce mountain fighters. Abdel Krim had twenty thousand men with modern weapons; the French nearly seven hundred thousand. The war continued for another year. In April, Abdel Krim was forced to surrender.

It was fortunate for France, and for Morocco too, that during the first few years of the protectorate a truly great and generous man, Marshal Louis Lyautey, was placed in command. He was totally dedicated to the task of establishing a French presence in the area, but he also learned to love the people he was administering and to honor those he was fighting. To this day Moroccans remember him with respect. Unfortunately his views of the "protector's" role were not shared by most of the men who followed him as representatives of France. The protectorate was to become in fact a colony.

With the end of armed resistance, the national struggle was taken over by the young intellectuals living in the cities. They too were taught French and thus enabled to absorb the ideals of freedom and independence from French books.

The nationalists appealed to the solidarity of the Arab world with which they had become largely identified. The French sought to counter the threat by trying to promote antagonism between the Berbers of the mountains and the countryside and the Arab-oriented youth in the cities. The attempt did not succeed, mainly because a distinguished Sultan, Sidi Mohammed ben Youssef, had succeeded in rallying most of the country around the throne. He was both a temporal and a religious leader. In his first capacity he was little more than a figurehead; but in his second, his power was great indeed. The sovereign had enemies and antagonists, including a number of pashas (regional governors) who owed their position to France. The most famous and influential was El Glaoui, Pasha of Marrakesh.

During World War II, Moroccan troops fought for the Allies. In November 1942 the Allied armies landed in North Africa. The French had been defeated by the Germans and their prestige was at a low ebb. The Allies recognized the authority of General de Gaulle, for whom, however, President Franklin D. Roosevelt had very little sympathy. When the President reached Casablanca for the famous conference that bears its name, he asked to meet the Sultan and he assured him of American support for Moroccan independence.

The French tried to re-establish the situation that existed before the war, but it was too late. The Sultan was now completely committed to the nationalist cause. The French reacted by exiling him and his family to the island of Madagascar, and put on the throne a new Sultan, whom the population rejected. Two years later, in November 1955, Mohammed and the royal family were brought back to Morocco. Shortly afterward—March 2, 1956—France proclaimed the sovereignty and independence of Morocco. Spain did likewise the following month. Mohammed took the title of King and moved toward the creation of a constitutional monarchy.

No sooner was independence proclaimed than relations with France were put to a severe test. In October 1956, three leaders of the Algerian Front of National Liberation, including future President Ben Bella, were kidnapped on a Moroccan airliner by the French. The King recalled his Ambassador in Paris, but also intervened personally to prevent reprisals against the French

81

*Mausoleum in Rabat dedicated to the memory of Mohammed V, the first King of independent Morocco, a ruler much beloved by his people.*

still living in Morocco. Relations with France were later re-established.

King Mohammed died in 1961 and was followed on the throne by his son, who took the title of Hassan II. The young King, a person of great intelligence, soon instituted a personal rule. He is unquestionably popular, most Moroccans being devoted to the monarchy. However, many of the young intellectuals who in the past were exclusively concerned with the issue of independence are now anxious to achieve a greater measure of equality and democracy for their country. Some of them fear that the King, being immensely wealthy, does not favor basic changes they consider urgent. Following a number of attempts on his life, some organized by army officers, the King's rule became increasingly personal and unresponsive to pressures in favor of greater political liberalization. Having rejected Western progress during the centuries of its self-defeating isolationism, Morocco is far behind most modern countries in development. Whether this situation will be corrected through intelligent planning or a violent explosion, only the future will tell.

MARIO ROSSI was born in Venice, Italy. He attended the University of Venice, the University of Geneva, and the New School for Social Research in New York, from which he received a Ph.D. in political science. A frequent contributor to various magazines, he is the author of *The Third World: The Nonaligned Countries and the World Revolution.* For many years he covered the United Nations, first for the *Christian Science Monitor* and then for the *St. Louis Post-Dispatch.* He lives in New York City, where he devotes himself to writing.